The Book of Moons

Published by La Pus Press 2022

First published in the United Kingdom in 2022 by
La Pus Press
Wales

A CIP record for this book is available from the British Library

ISBN: 9781739947927

cover design and illustration by Keone

The Book of Moons

Keone

La Pus Press

Contents

For Libby, sharer of dreams & poems

The truth is myth

We don't control stories

They tell themselves

The Dreamings Of

Stop me if you've heard this already. One of the first dreams I remember is sitting in the back of an open jeep at the entrance to a block of flats near where we lived, being chased by a Tyrannosaurus Rex. I was probably around 6 when I had this dream in 1980, years before off-road vehicles and Jurassic Park were things that would shape the collective imagination. Though some people might consider dreams to be ephemeral, this one is as vivid now as when it first showed itself.

Dreams that stood out from my teenage years had a similar sense of threat. The one of a shark rising from the plughole in the bath was definitely related to watching Jaws. But less traceable and more eerie was a dream about two black-clothed burglars, faceless and silent, running from the open front door of the house I grew up in with my mother in Cardiff. It was the silence that was most disturbing; a lack of explanation; like witnessing a crime that could never be solved.

During most of my twenties I was in a deeply committed and self-destructive polyamorous relationship with both marijuana and tobacco. As a result my days took on a dreamy quality while my nights were a fog where little of note took place. It was only after consciously uncoupling that I realised how the rolling anaesthetic of being stoned managed to destroy both my dreams and the capacity to act on them.

When the dreams returned they did so with a ferocity that woke me up, (screaming, damp with sweat, shaking) and changed the trajectory of my life. This particular dream saw me running from someone I knew was going to kill me. I was near my secondary school and found what I thought was a matchless hiding spot under a bridge until I felt a presence behind me and turned to see a large, bald-headed man launch at me with a spoon to cut out my heart. This dream punctured the narrative that I wheeled out: how I was all Zen about dying. It helped me to expand my meditation from mind-stilling to mind-exploring, and led me to start working with the one creature I feared more than any other: Spider.

This dream was the beginning of my experience of the shamanic tool of journeying. It led me to embark on a path that, amongst many things, opened doors to a more conscious awareness of other realities. There were two further dreams directly related to dying. During the days after the second, where Abigail from school announced she was also going to kill me, I would journey with Spider (who sounded like Michael Caine), until I faced my fear, surrendered to the Mother of all Spiders, was consumed and allowed to pass through her, initiated and transformed. It was after this I received the third dream in the sequence. Even though I was in a lift as it shook and knew it was about to plummet, I felt at peace with dying. It was at that point the lift steadied itself, the doors opened, and on I stepped.

Contrary to what's been written, not all my dreams have been about being killed. I've had several experiences of déjà vu where I felt certain the events being lived had already taken place in a dream. They've not been particularly grand or dramatic - one saw me standing outside a house I was staying in for a few weeks while planes streaked overhead. But their importance was what they suggested about the relationship between our waking and dreaming realities. While dreams come on different levels – from clearing the psychic debris of the day, to offering symbolic puzzles and revealing hidden aspects of ourselves – they also seem to offer us visions of days not yet lived; like trailers for films we later sit through and think 'I remember this bit'.

I'm always interested to hear other people's dreams, especially those that recur. My recurring dreams involve tidal waves. I've had many variations on them, but what they all share is a resolution to the impending peril. Sometimes the wave freezes.

Or it stays eternally rotating. Or I dive through. Always I wake feeling there's nothing to fret about; that everything works out in the end.

This collection evolved out of a practice, begun some years ago, of writing down my dreams. The more I journeyed and the further I continued with my healing, the clearer my dreams grew. At first these dream records were scratchy, little more than shopping lists in reverse. But over the last decade I noticed something happen. The more I wrote, the clearer the dreams became, the more fluent the writings appeared as a result. I learned to distinguish between jolly, mixed-up romps and more significant carriers; focusing on writing down those dreams that jolted me awake, in which there seemed to be some medicine that I was being asked to record. None of the dreams had titles. Instead I would write them up with the date they came through. I wasn't sure the purpose in recording them, beyond personal record, until I woke from one and as I wrote it down realised it was taking the form of a poem. Almost immediately I got the message where we were going with these.

Our Celtic ancestors knew the value of dreams. Like many indigenous folx across time, they understood multidimensionality and the existence of more than a single reality. For them, dreams were a different, helpful reality that wove together the ordinary reality of waking life and the non-ordinary reality of altered consciousness. Living well in one reality meant attending to how we live in others.

It was our ancestors who also named the different moons of the year, both to mark the seasons and also to honour trees, plants and animals. As I brought the dreams together I noticed how many of them came through at either the time of the dark moon, where the old moon has vanished and the new moon is yet to emerge, or under the three-night spell of the full moon. The title of the collection, like the poems contained within, wrote itself.

For someone who now goes by the name given to them on a slip of paper by a woman in a dream, The Book of Moons is our child.

Keone
Wales
2022

Ash Moon

A large festival at a seafront village is ready to start
Grandmother Sun is on the verge of a big change
saying

Share your moon dreams
Grow with the moon
They are strongest just after full

I see a crystal round her neck

Cycling out of the village past a large old building
where people can no longer afford to live or work

A tower above the town
Red garnet & obsidian in bands
like a skyscraper or thin temple

Water levels have risen
soaking the roads
Cycling past giant puddles
wondering whether to catch a bus or train
then cycling back to the festival just as it starts

A man has locked his bike
but the lock has been stolen
& all its clever complexities turn against him

Asking him
Now what was the point of that lock again

Always We Find a Way

A chubby handsome man is lost on the underground
& doesn't know whether he wants Victoria or Brick Lane

We go for kofta
which he has to leave as he has tickets for a show
He invites me along
even though his husband is somewhere

Plus he has a gun tucked into the waist of his shorts

I say
Listen if that bullet is for me let's at least sit down and eat
Maybe yes a bottle of wine
so I can dine with my assassin

Elsewhere
I'm helping a child of the aristocracy
with his colours and words

His father has a priceless carafe of something with 0% alcohol
& colourless
He asks if I'd mind
having tap water
as his liquid is really rather special

The family tries to enlighten me at how marriage works for them
which seems incredibly complicated
but actually
the mother stresses testily

is to make sure we marry other rich families in order
as though I'm simple

There is a drama with a vintage bar of family soap
& I've clearly done something that betrays my peasant blood

We go to the beach
which isn't far
& swim a little way out
to where the waves start

Swimming back
each wave that bounces off the coast grows higher
Threateningly so

Yet always we find a way
below the breaking crest
to breathe

Birth Moon

Homunculus is going to kill me
& film it
That will be the end
Or will it?

She doesn't want the square plate I say I'll leave
& why should she
with everything tidied up for dispatch

Trying very hard to explain how
in Sussex
the land artist scraped back grass
to let chalk paths glow in moonlight
& repeating *limestone*
wrongly

The train from west to east is struggling with floods
Death would & wouldn't be bloody
would & wouldn't be live

With a palette knife
the rising squares of houses
& their shiny slate roofs
make a chain of sugared bites
munching up the hill

Mourning Moon

A house by a lake
The waters are rising
They have risen past the banks of the lake
& are now lapping at the door

In the toilet
sewage is falling from the ceiling

We sail in a boat on a world of water
to a faded fairground
where old people are waiting to ride

Memento Mori

I mean not so much a poem as a picture
Skulls on black cloth

An elderly queer artist
Bacon mixed with Hockney & someone with a perm
looking like Brian Sewell

1970s posters being sloshed over with paste & brushed up
under bridges in Paris

A tea party of queens
One of them sobbing about love
& Barbara Cartland

& this view
of moon & sea

Photographing it
who knows where

Milk Moon

In the marshes
homeless without a sleeping bag
though there's a bag
bags even

A couple giving me a bed for the night
just one night mind
& there being some debate
as whether to bring the laminate into the office
where the single sofa bed is
or carpet

Oh carpet
she said
would get terrible dirty

Leaving in a thunder storm
under a wide high sky
& being struck by lightning
who's a goddess
lifting me right off the floor

On Strumble Head

Near the coast where the ferry goes
at a fish & chip place

A drunk man is in these big toilets
with fireplaces you can walk into & sofas

He's too drunk to drive so we say to him
Rest
Stay
Let us drive you

Knowing then the need of men
to talk to other men

Lighting a fire the sacred way
Being paid even to be firelighter of the place

The wood store has coal in it
Feeling confused by the coal

Amongst the kindling
small jewels of wood
One in the shape of a cat

The woman in charge shows it to another man

It's not finished
we say

Blue

It was ridiculous really
A ship with a flight of stairs so long
it went all the way down
to the silent dark of the ocean

A flight of stairs that glowed phosphorescent blue
like ice in the abyss

Yet we walked them
convinced not only of their reality
but all the lessons they proved
Until we were miles down & cold alone

It was only when we climbed back
into the ordinary cruise of the ship
that we saw how crazy the whole exercise was
How like a film or a joke
Something done with mirrors & ready gullible heads

Even then
a sense of having seen the impossible
like miners or moon-walkers

Standing at the edge of nothing
On the pause of a staircase
made of blue ice

Being let in on a secret
no one else believed

Blackthorn Moon

At my mother's house
I'm scrubbing her bedroom carpet
because she's old now & can't do it

Through the adjoining doors
I hear she has a lodger

In an old communal farm building
there are lots of familiar faces
& chairs needing to be put away

Tiptoeing out of a garden centre
so as not to disturb Polar Bear
as I move past from returning a chair

Of course Polar Bear is not asleep but awake
watching
staying restful & gently observant
like a cat

Seals

At the beach there are lots of seals splashing
getting everyone's attention

When we see them next they all merge
into one single seal
& the next moment separate out again

Donald Trump's house is right on the seafront in Brighton
There are massive waves
which imply he's in a permanent state of defence
but we think
well he can always move

In the sea
many sharks merge into a single shark
as the seals have done

Waving at zebras on a boat docking
& smiling at a woman who says (telepathically)
Keep connecting

This woman
nodding at the seal that is all the seals
says
Please don't tell anyone about this
She just got very excited & couldn't help herself

& us saying
It's the coolest thing ever

Harvest Moon

There is so much blood

I'm drinking it with a fellow
other vampire
on the fringes

Look – we're just trying our best
to navigate safely
kindly
& survive

Uninvited

In a department store
finding an expensive body cream reduced
with a big cat on it

Upstairs
no one wants to serve me
This one guy upping & leaving
saying he'll find someone else
but no one coming

I wait
After a while go downstairs
replace everything & leave
telling an assistant manager
I'm not wanted here

Outside in the city
trying to find somewhere to stay
Ending up in a ruined cement hotel
A boy is with me but he's drunk
& just wants a hole

The provocatrix is organizing a club night
I know I don't want to go
before realising I'm not invited

There's a handful of party confetti on a desk
Throwing it
Feeling it tinkle down the back

Troxy

Flying across the roof of the Troxy Bingo Hall
an old 1930s theatre in Limehouse
full of drag queens

Kylie is here in a black wig
& Katya

Speaking to a drag queen who asks my name
& when I tell her she says
What was your previous name?

Outside in the car park I'm having a piss
It's deserted except for one man in the shadows
Back inside, I'm speaking with a boy
whose bag is woven like my skirt
We speak of fashion as we return outside
where it is now rammed

The boy says his name is Cheston, King of Israel
before taking out a gun & shooting me
The bullet hits the phone in my chest pocket & I play dead

As he announces why I have to die
I grip him by the throat & his gun falls

Don't kill him
the drag queens say
surrounding him
We'll take it from here

Last Quarter

They are vampires

Sexy, modern like a reality show in LA
but still out to take

Here's a young black girl
Hero
Defender

She has a gold ring

Later in some sort of hotel
I take the last bit of cake

although I left it on the table intentionally

What?

The gardener is in the polytunnel growing... what?
Plants? Tomatoes? Weed?

Outside there's a party crowded with adults
all talking by the bar
but I'm not part of that

Instead I'm photographing the ruined façade of a monastery
which is near a courtyard of council flats
blending in with a school

Marian the mermaid is in the vaults of a church
swimming in its pool
while a guide shows off huge caverns of alcohol

I realise this is home & I'm waiting for my man to come
while watching the telly with housemates

Someone has invented Tavarys
which is a nickel-coated metal & strong
Apparently

I am feeling way too hot in these tights so take them off

The door goes & someone else answers
My man comes up the stairs

Why I feel like I have to put my clothes back on again
is anyone's guess

Again, Crossing

In a town square
that could be any bombed-out post-war square
with Wilkos and a TK Maxx

Asking a passer-by where we are
Him saying
Macclesfield
& me thinking
I've never been to Macclesfield

Asking him where
for the short period of time I have left
should I see?

Him pointing to the left of a map
& saying
There
Around Mouse Street

Walking west
down a candy sweet street
ending in a narrow stairwell that goes up
then down
to cross a train line

Realising everything is further away
so running, then becoming a train
then seated on the train thinking
There is so much world to see

Approaching a place full of Victorian arcades
being done up into shops selling ceiling roses
wall cornices & other period moulding styles

In one shop
this couple comes in to offer
a swatch of egg-shaped paper
The shop designer
asks if they have a bungalow
like it's a matter of life or death

I walk down the street past a pharmacy & bank
thinking
it's half past four
how much more time do I have?

Crossing the road
I see a man with long dreads & silver skin
performing yoga postures

Feeling the habit to look at him
but knowing I need to not disturb him
Still sensing him wobble
though I am most definitely not looking

Much

Instead I'm walking back up the high street
on the other side of the road
with its supermarket all ordinary

Crossing once again at the top
saying
I've known what it is to be wrong
I've stolen & I've cheated

& feeling it clean
The ownership

Clean and flat
like the sort of stone
that skips over water

Edge

At the edge of the ocean
we come together
to sing
to burn
to offer sand
& release

How do we do this now
after so long forgetting?

No one knows separately
but together we help each other back
with arms escorting across mud

She's almost a sister
but as she departs on her rugby tour
in the other car
she won't hug
Not fully

Bends her head down like a ram
butting the heart

Only after her grandfather passes
years later
does she welcome us back

We are worrying blu tack off a baize board

Wolf Moon

On a picnic bench with a boy in summer
Stealing their hash
while they slip away for a moment
even though we have more than enough in our tin

Trying to whistle our innocence
as they come back & suggest we walk
around a cloistered garden

They say
I think we need to have a little talk, don't you
& feeling frightened
because we know

The boy shimmers
shifts into a divinity
& it's like school again
being caught at the back of the sports block
by Mr Jenkins

Owning up and throwing away the stash
in the ornamental flower beds
Then watching a film about the curative properties of yoghurt

Giving our friend the last blim
& seeing his paintings
This one in particular
with rainbow stripes like curtains
& a golden turtle

Fasting Moon

Together with my twin flame in a flat above a beach
I have to get down to the sand
He holds a pink towel so I might swing into the flat below
& use their stairs

From the beach I can see a simpler way for him
& point to the next door flat
which has stairs down

Then we're back in his flat
hanging out
He's making food for us
I notice how much more well-stocked his kitchen is
compared with last time

He still has bags of sweeties, yes
but also bowls of fruit & crackers
It feels abundant
Healthy

We talk easily
There's no desire or want or sadness
just a familiar unity

I say
It wasn't so much that I felt electricity with you
As being with you showed the electricity I had within myself

Rise

A warehouse space with wooden floors
like a yoga studio
We're here to practice

In a garden being chased by a boy
Needing to not be caught by him
so hiding as a tree

The sky turning weird
like an electric storm

Us
Many of us
Coming together to do this work

Is it battle or ballet?
Sensing the fight to come but saying
It can also be a dance

In a city estate
full of towers
a woman saying of a young boy who died
He really wanted to be with you

The sight of a wild flower garden border
Knowing we are here to shine exactly as we shine
& help everything around us bloom

We rise by helping everyone rise

Chips

As we speak
the dead tree on the lawn is being eaten
eviscerated in time lapse
from the inside out
at speed

Owl comes to feed on the insects
Or is it Gull

There's a book for you

Searching through the bag
I find one with comments
you've written over
(*cold / stiff / frozen*)
crossing off the words you don't like

We are guests in someone else's house
& generously they've left the TV on
playing a familiar film

Other copies need to be posted
to faeries in wild parts
one of whom is in a new build
though the postwoman
knows for a fact that the street isn't occupied yet
& he's squatting

The other we've not heard of

which makes me wonder
why we're going to the trouble of posting him anything

At the bar
you order a portion of chips
to share
& then change it to a portion each

The barman brings one across that is half eaten
while the next is battered in mayonnaise
but at least he swaps our bundle of coins for a fiver

& you agree with a plate each
as we're both starving

Worm Moon

In a student house
a purple-bodied spider is spitting from its bum

I worry for my cat

There's a hedgehog inside
& I'm thinking
Why are you inside?

The middle room of the house is large
If we remove a false ceiling it'll be great for meditation

Builders arrive to start the renovation
but I tell them to stop

They say
Shyrdak legend says
to stop a job means someone dies

Saying
Don't stop then
but maybe try a different house

Being with my partner
who's excited we're doing this together
Seeing their face & thinking
Really? Them?

Ice Moon

There's a party happening at an empty house
with walls of coloured blocks

A piece of graffiti is being painted over
& the rooms upstairs at the back have no windows

The party is hosted by a gay couple
sorting drinks for everyone

As we're not drinking we go outside
where we see the house on a hill surrounded by fields
& a grove of laburnum trees

One of the trees has been used to hang people
& a queue of unquiet spirits occupies the space

We turn to this one woman
who is gripping onto a swing
tight & scared
& ask her
where's your mum

We watch her shift her head
realise
& release

A feeling of lightness comes in place
Like a star-shaped piece finding its star-shaped hole
& vanishing

Home

In the churchyard there is loss & sadness
A pruned apple tree
Marriage gone
Baby gone

We are at your house in the backroom
We need to light a candle
any candle
You have several
though they are old & dusty
their wicks smothered in wax

Everything about this feels ready

We come to you in the front room
All our friends are there & we say
We can do this
Not *I*
We

Your husband looks exhausted & says
How much is this going to cost us?
We tell him it isn't about the money

It's about fire in the place
Or if not (as the chimney won't draw)
plenty of candles
A bucket of water
Earth

Yes, yes, incense you're right
by the staff

As we speak
your eyes light with a passion
that is & isn't you
& you say quite slow
deliberate
I do not want to leave her
before reaching to grip my throat

But this is we not me
There is a circle of light & a circle of us
Our tribe
our friends
(one especially hugging your back)
& beyond

Those with us who make the rainbow bridge
who with limitless compassion
open a portal for you to live on
as pure spirit & continue

Those who say

Her body is not for you
Her sadness will heal
Her void is light – lit

Here we all are in circle
helping you home

Mother's Moon

The headmistress of the Mystery School
had passed & we found her with a folder
at a gateway

Speaking with her
asking where she was
& her saying
I don't know

What can you see?
She closes her eyes
& then it's a sort of darkness & falling
& she cries

As we land on a hill
a gull baby is crying its way out of an egg

We have come to this land before
many times for gatherings & look
here are photos

The herbalist is saying
It was very demanding
They the gods were tough

Adding
It wasn't the gods who made the demands
but those who served them

Making cut-out pictures & when framing them
all the parts falling off

Swallowing the copper ring
Feeling it move inside
Knowing there'll be shit to go through
but clearing out & being cleansed

Collecting insects & eggs from the floor
& one of them
like a bee skeleton
moving & screaming

Not dead

Like the mouse the cat caught yesterday

Father's Moon

Yes it was about death
specifically mine & doing it

Everyone was there as actors
like extras to the scene

The last big dick
that I was & wasn't ready for
that broke me
I shat all over
like a cloud breaking

There was a church
Figures gathered
waiting for a sign they could start wailing

It was like video footage already existed
& was waiting to be played

At the exact moment

I was riding a deer & on my last breath lifted
joined with my always cat
& rode in expanding leaps
over that roundabout
by Dilwyn Street
in Swansea

stopping

to help the medium's fingers
barely touching the sand in her bowl
move & say
Love to everyone

before returning to the tableau at the church
to see the other actors
& wave

Magic

Magic we are
leaping over trees, buildings
in one spring

Dancing on the tops of conifers
Giggling like children

I can tell you're Queen Elizabeth
from how you said *marchpane*
& ate the apostles first

Here be phantoms
skeletons doing limbo
at railway crossings

It's a gift this
True say
bouncing right as high beside

Yet we know we'll end up one day
parched old bones
dancing like xylophones
out of life

There are others who aren't yet sure
how any of this is happening

They're the ones we're here to tell

Pink Moon

Two dancers meet again
at a fish market in Brixton

One says to the other
We never had the chance to get to know each other

The other turns away
cross but smirking
returning when beckoned

The first one says they're going to New York
to research a book on Rumi
& asks the other what they think

A dream for fools
The other replies

How are you coping with being ignored?

Long Nights Moon

The girl with cropped hair says she wants to make it
simple enough for an eight year-old to understand
But we are dealing with toddlers in charge of nuclear arsenals

& yet

There are those aspects of the despised
(communities, independent, land-reclaiming, state-negating)
that sing

In a large room like an abandoned office
we are trying to make home

He wants the picnic table gone
but even if we had a truck it wouldn't fit
How about we move it outside for the school kids to smoke at?

We arrange lighting as the bulbs dim

You & I find each other again
embracing
as in that old photo

I share
You weep apologies for not waiting
& I join you
for not being sorted quick enough

There are sketches too

Ophiuchus

I'm in your flat
but ill-at-ease
as though I'm squatting

A deranged man goes to see a pregnant woman
& ends up throwing a door at her

I say to them both
Imagine if you were a young child & witnessed this
while chaperoning the cracked man out

Elsewhere there's a dance hall with folk
doing a performance piece & then a poem
about loss

Moving to San Francisco
not because the loss goes
but because here is a place where it can live

Hay Moon

I was taking a bus to my old bay
further along the coast

This was supposed to be a trip for us both
only you'd let me know sorry
you weren't feeling it

I went on alone
around the craggy bends
where suddenly sea would appear
turquoise & inviting

I knew I would be okay
Would walk back on the coastal path
Was even now closer than I'd ever been
to not putting my heart in hands
that couldn't hold

The Beach

You look young
like I'm child-minding for the day
Tight black curls
Chocolate skin

We're at the beach & the sand is like flour
Light as face powder

You extend a foot
like a ballerina
& I paint your nails gold
First right
Then left

Gold
Cocoa sand
& a feeling like copper satin over everything

If you were here now we'd be kissing

In Nain's Flat

You come over & we make love
Completing

Of course it feels different
because thirty nearly years

Your husband is a logistic for you to deal with
as I spill down the stairs
to tell Charles and his two doggish friends
that I am otherwise engaged
& will not be taking a walk round the block

Your son though

I am ready to move up the road
then your mother is with us
& we are making a chicken pie

One part already cooked for the baking
when we decide to add another
raw & bleeding like an accident

I remember thinking
the timings will be off now
as we lay what feels like kidneys, liver and the heart
along the top to brown & crust

Taliesin

Near the coast
but having to leave by going out to sea

As soon as this is decided
it feels like it needs to be secret
like it isn't allowed

& someone is already policing us
to bring us back

As we swim away
they follow

So we shift

First into a chameleon
slipping back into a house
Then a cat, then a bird
a dragon, a flea

& being on the wind
flying
outside the law

Meeting others who are ready
to set the destroying churches ablaze

Not having a name
Not even a body

When the sirens come
we are just another overlooked ladybird
amid the weeds
tucked into a friend's breast pocket
watching over the hem

Fortress of the Moon

London
The tops of trees are burning

A Maori man is ululating
bringing down the walls of St Paul's

Strawberry Moon

The major standing for prime minister
leans against the door frame with a pencil moustache
while the interviewer realises he's fucked it up
& tries to start again

In the orange dining hall
the staff are eating
It isn't the place to come wandering
even as a tourist

The woods are drier now
Puddles barely present

An artist & her daughter
are smoking in their run-around car

The artist had to give back her camper van
which saddens her
Also there is a problem
with her father-in-law's memorial stone

The car is up on concrete steps
with a piece of fencing
as a last gift from my mother
who wanted me to have something useful

In the supermarket
the newspapers are all about
a famous impersonator of Mrs Thatcher

who's died

At the bus stop we stand
while several buses pass
catching none of them

In Manchester

The loud boomer couple are ordering food

I go for a walk
find a poetry book in a charity shop
then go to a reading in a giant hall
crowded with people

George Michael is upstairs playing
before an intimate audience
Only this is a different one
Not THE George Michael

The spy doctor is there
Silver-haired now
I say
I've been thinking of you & knew that when we met
we would walk into each other

We hug
He's with his boyfriend
which is surprising
as when we'd last seen each other
he'd been straight

We say goodbye
He's off to an airport but isn't travelling on
He prefers to stop there

I leave on foot

aiming for a train station into the wilds
trying to find the path

It leads into a house
where each room gets smaller than the last
but walls can be pushed
& actually the key is to rise to another level

It's here that a post-apocalyptic group
is living in abandoned train cars

The girls are friendly
One goes through my bag
I say
I wouldn't do that if I were you
sounding like a complete dick

There's that poetry book
Seeing the price of it on the back

Remembering when we had the money for it

First Quarter

There is the standing up
& talking about this old age dying
How it comes back to the tailors & dreamers
Thumb   foot   yard   span
(only not remembering their names)

There is the sound of my mother
alive to the changes
& showing how they link

The city of lights
is a candle embossed with a gate

We are not in the city
but the fringes of it stretch

News of a helicopter landing close by
The way the signals bend the fig tree
palms down

But also friends are here
like the mushroom man
So we gather to work out
where is a good field for us all to eat
seeing as many are now arriving

& this phone
the one in your hand even now
Put it away more

Omy

With some other gays on a Titanic-like boat
It has struck & we all know what's coming

Trying to work out what to take
(Leggings, waterproofs
an inflatable mattress that will float...)
& where on the boat to jump off from

Later
Walking out of a house with Omy

A girl
A chair
Inevitable scatter cushions
Letting off a flare for help

We stop
& she says
Don't underestimate the enormous shock
you've gone through

Hunger Moon

Creeping around a room
so as not to wake the lizzies

some of whom are moving into the modern age
by evolving into robots
& are nearby

Police checks all across the city

Coup

A right wing coup has been organized for tomorrow

They have a salute & are gathering
to begin removing people

We know who we are

A man says
*Someone went to work at the end of my table
& never came back*

Walking the streets
with padded chair backs

Telling people face to face
not online

That's why we're on the street

Moving careful through the chaos
thinking
At least now it's out in the open

Cold Moon

In my grandmother's kitchen
the eggs sit on a bench
tucked out of sight & mind

It's only when a sister asks for headphones
to play a prank on the singer from Simple Minds
(who's joined the tree top rebellion)
that it starts

The eggs need a cable that has gone

Suddenly we see how precious they are
life & food
& fragile

The garden witch is there reminding us
like my grandmother
that we need to return to a time of spell
Of ritual & protection

When the builder whistles in we are on it
defending the eggs from his clumsy dusty charge
Then it's the B&B guests
who are really so much more

Cast the circle
Cast the circle

Air   Fire   Water   Earth

Elder Moon

Princess Diana is trapped in a place of jewels & palaces
but no love

We're in a house with someone
who makes our difference feel like madness
until we are shut in & weeping

It's the primary school teacher
- we see her again & again
& each meeting feels more like a message -
who helps us break free

Later
in a shop full of large canvases
the black negative space is visible
like seams running through all our landscapes

Wanting to be in a place by the sea far from everyone
Also wanting to be close to a little shop

Finding ourselves in London
at what feels like a burial site for women with
above it
a sanctuary for refugees

It is the women who have suffered throughout this age
& continue to
We are singing now
but need to let our sleeping sisters rest

Ar Y Coed

Wise woman
Water whisperer
Stone charmer
Say

There is room for you here
& it is your room

Energy is a living being

When you ask the bees to come out from their caves
be sure why you are asking
For them to have a home
or as a trick
Cheap

Welsh is the old language of charm
At the water's rim
there is ceremony
Salt water
Where Shark swim

Not the metal head of an axe

You know this
You remember this
We will show you

Like magnets that attract

Moon Time

Looking for seeds in Hackney
A gardener with big hands is working out moon time
collecting seeds at her fullest

The black & white kitten purring friendly
grows into a big ginger Tom

This land is now owned by a rich family
raising pigs to kill them & collecting art

They've brought it from an old mother
who welcomes us but looks sad
saying
Our land has been taken over
& we are now tenants

She tells us that she's been away
& when we ask her
where
she expands to the size of a mountain & says
Peru

Then she holds our palm & says
There it is
On your hand

while her daughter keeps brushing
her long auburn hair straight
in her room

Journey Moon

Being in the docklands
Needing to get somewhere
but not getting the DLR

It appears I'm a lesbian
handling a businessman's yacht
flying over water & First World War memorial towers

Now I'm at your flat
making you a morning coffee
even though there are only jugs in your cupboard
no cups or mugs

Your mother is doing yoga
Or wanting to
but needing a thicker mat

Somebody else is trying to sell her an inflatable

Sometimes
we say
we need to be on the earth

Moon Goddess

There is a fridge balanced on empty take away cartons

The wild women are here

At Aldgate station
Nearly missing the last tube
but catching a special service
that looks like something from the 1940s

There are patrols on the street
Older women with rods in tights on view

Mothers too
Spinning threads about Spider
who sacrifices herself
so her children can have their first meal

The Moon Goddess is on the sofa with moons in her hair
She says
Haven't we met?

A daughter
Children
What's stopping you?

Come on Daniel

She says it kindly
but it makes me feel sad

& I want to shout back
Fuck you all

She smiles

The wood witch is nearby
rubbing our hand
as we wake gently up

Blood Moon

Moon over bay
with a rim of lights
like a crescent

A painting of San Francisco
Shapes looking like vacant parking garages
empty honeycomb cells

Meaning the ideas have gone
a sister says
excited

Berries on trees
The scissor witch wants to be close & welcoming
but with secateurs & a hunger to cut

Her saying
I understand because you are like me, child
Scorpio in your 11th house

Sorting Moon

Science has to start somewhere

We manage to help the woman
at the tube station
get her money
but the orange scatter cushion has gone & can't be found
not even in the oversized plastic hamper
of all the other unloved cushions
left behind on the station platform

I wonder whether he might have it
but in his flat it's all purple, navy & blue in oblongs
& I count at least six spare beds

He's too busy for any of this
coding games with polyamorous central characters
who can shapeshift
Too busy even for the blowjob I think I have to give him

Because it's daytime not pub-time & daytime is work-time

He's happier with the out-of-town shops
the new estates on the ring road
& needs to get back to the game

What about those who aren't allowed in the game?
What about hags & witches?
What games for them?
Those who are told they aren't allowed to belong

Caravan

There are people in small squares
digging holes for pools

If they'd only take the walls down
their pools would join
& there'd be more room to swim

More room
like the crumbling estate
that needs not so much money
as love

Vans come circling like wagons
There are people waiting
wanting to find their way back to the land
To help
To live

13

The wise woman wears an orb of water
on her brow

A pure circle
containing rainbows

Before us
arranged around cards
hand-painted
on her altar
the suit of snakes

Thirteen
I ask

Because it's you

The Smallest Thing

Being at her family's house
& their internet being down

Volunteering to go to the card shop down the street
to get a selection for them

She says
Please get
Moose
Frogs
Fishes
& the Art of Greece

The shop is a terraced house
with a plump queer man in metallic face paint
purplish
& a kimono

Inside
his card selection is small
& high up

We talk of the virus
& he says

We knew we had to stop but couldn't
so something else had to stop us
& it ended up being the smallest thing

Snow Moon

In the computer game
on the top floor
there was a bridge
which we were banned from crossing
because of Covid

We won by beaming out love

Love   Love   Love
while we died

Love all the way
that's how we survived

Then we moved to a community in Berlin
& jumped in the bath for joy

Courting Moon

We were looking at the news
& suddenly it seemed like the most unbelievable rubbish

A tiny face that on its own made no sense
You had to zoom out & see
it applied to the whole system

We were chatting online
& where you were
the sky was ridiculous with stars
Clear and dizzying

You had a telescope & we said
Please let's look through that instead

& what it looked like was an elastic band
twisted in the middle
showing all the stars not as we see them
spread out like a blanket
but focused & narrow through the elongated hoops

Somehow we were seeing them
flattened out across the sky from Earth
& somewhere else
dead perhaps
viewing the whole figure of eight from away

It was compelling
The stars all ways

& us
together again

Nearly

Far from the rubbish of news
Dazzled at the planets
& where they sat
Burning

Seed Moon

Feel it move through the world
& through us

Gateways that have been closed are open
& all we want to do is giggle

There is pleasure now
joyous & ancient as the picture of the dark goddess
dancing on her god
on the cover of that book
in a second-hand shop

Walking through the streets in love with everyone
Feeling myself move to take a man
Any man
Every man
Take him by the horn and feel him
Urgent

Weakening
Uncoiling
Writhing

What else is needed now
than to make small circles at the font of his head
& feel him constantly wet

Willow Moon

The news channels keep talking about traffic jams & blocks
but in these temples
gays, women & children are here to dance
& make love

Nothing is blocking
There is only flow

Everywhere you look
people
helping each other
reaching out in circle after circle
to hold each other's hands

Hare Moon

In the garden we are here
wizards & wise women

It is approaching the time when they're due to arrive
& we're spread out like a blanket
woven across fields

It's like a cross between a monastery & a rave

When did you last hear the call?
someone asks
& I think of the fishing village I was born in
& a compilation from Café del Mar playing in cloisters

They arrive
Around the garden we have potions to help

We are dancing
There is a sense of everything coming together
Of threads that stretch back to first mother
being felt again

A mother is here with her child
although the child is elsewhere

& we feel drawn together
like a great *aha*
like two horsemen have come at once

He comes to me & introduces himself as
Anthony
with hands as old as the moon

Passes me the gold-threaded back of a chair
like a lyre

There is panic in a corner as a woman has collapsed
Is being loved & tended by other women

There is flapping
a scratching of invisible wings & claws

Her son
someone calls
Where is her son?

Outside we turn
weaving close to the ground
through summer grass
on a small bank
near apple trees

We know the pavement is sentient
& the grass magical

We sense that time coming
when we remember
how connected we are

The old queen is rolling a smoke

All around the sound is of six o'clock in the morning
a club track that has no time
only a noise
& won't end

We say

Now is the time
Let us sing

& from nowhere comes Mama Cass

Stars shining bright above
Dream a little dream of me

Star

The artist is upset
reversing backwards

She wanted to draw a star & says she didn't do it right

Says
It was up to you to draw it, bring it down
Says
Look at all the ways those people helped you

A school of whales is in a bay
Loads of boats are trying to keep them out to sea
but still they come in

A man turns & says
isn't it spectacular?

Answering him
Idiot! They're going to die

The next thing
there are mortuary slabs on the sand
all their bodies laid out

& I'm wailing
saying
I did this
Because I didn't draw the star

Call

I called
& a Maori elder
(Ancestor? Father?)
appeared
saying

You summoned me

Old Moon

We destroyed the skyscrapers to money greed
& inequality

Only with the magic of the ancestors
With love for those who had been crippled & belittled
& by blowing up the bombs the place had created to safe itself

We moved through the golden cells
of the banks of information & surveillance
like a cat
disguised as the most irrelevant

But the gates opened
because of the ancestors
because the chi said
Let it be so
on the screens

What we saw was a dark green eye
in the Middle Lands
where their source was located

& coming out of the debris
through rubbled streets
where speakers repeated
How irrelevant you human scum

We reached our familia
Abuela was crying

& the family welcomed us back

They wouldn't find us here because
they wouldn't know where to look
Besides, the three-headed dog was on guard duty
with the black & red twins

It was here we could approach the shrine
& thank the ancestors
for all

Here
we would ask our cousins
for help to reach the temple
because this needed all of us

& to look after the cat
who said
I'm here to look after you, silly

Beaver Moon

It's about love
All of it

It's about the panel of raging youth
who want to be witnessed in their gender sex howl
& heard

It's about tears, feeling & showing them
whatever mess we make

It's about meeting the angry white man
who wants to bulldoze ahead
actually pushes you along the corridor
against the will of your wanted pace
& saying to him plain how it feels to be pushed
it feels aggressive
I feel forced

It's about the young son
who's been trying to speak with that dad for years
to have the space opened for him
to just be with him
for as long as he needs
at his pace

It's about love
for the wounded
For all of us
For all

Flower Moon

In this place
there's a whole lot of shit
in a bowl of water

But water clears it
so the shit vanishes

It is not about *I*
There is no *I* in *us*
It is about we
About spirit
About the collective
The cosmic

It is about intention
but also letting go of control

The daughter who wanted to murder her father
only succeeded in poisoning her mother

Love is not about appearances
See the soul & magic of life

We glow

Mead Moon

A room
A large smiling woman
robed in yellow

Windows open to the sea & beyond
the sunset

She has a table spread with sunflowers
butters
turmeric in milk

Everywhere peaches
grapefruit
honey

She smiles & waves her pendant of citrine saying

One day you will look out of your window
on years gone by & you will smile

You will always be surrounded by love
because you are love

Wort Moon

At a hotel in Austria
the music wizard has come to see us

A sense that this is where we end

He's coming to pay respects to a dead drag queen
& a family is upset
saying how important touch is

To touch & be touched

At the hotel
we're paying to stay
but getting breakfast for free

Outside is ivy all green
then a corridor
as you'd find in a student block

Going for a meal with a boy
like the twin from school
who worked in the hardware shop
at the crossroads

Sleeping with him to feel better

A woman saying
Really? Will it help?
Knowing it wouldn't

It was small
Not the right thing
But we've needed each other since we were six

A group of students signing
A girl showing us the sign for
milk
& it being like the one for *fucking*

Wanting tea with no milk
but ending up saying
Pizza please
& it feeling like cheating

Two women
Older
One complaining, the other arguing

One saying
I'll say I won't do it again
but I probably will

The other saying
I'll say I won't forgive you again
but I probably will

www.ingramcontent.com/pod-product-compliance
Lightning Source LLC
Chambersburg PA
CBHW030852090426
42737CB00009B/1206